Dancing Through Seafoam

INDIGORIVER
PUBLISHING

Dancing Through Seafoam

Poetic Reflections on the Circle of Life

DIANE SKYE GROPPER

Dancing Through Seafoam: Poetic Reflections on the Circle of Life

LCCN: 2025926649

ISBN: 978-1-969935-07-7 (paperback) 978-1-969935-08-4 (ebook)

Editors: Jennifer Casey, Deborah Froese

Cover and Interior Design: Emma Elzinga

Printed in the United States of America

First Edition

3 West Garden Street, Ste. 718

Pensacola, FL 32502

www.indigoriverpublishing.com

Ordering Information:

Quantity sales: Special discounts are available on quantity purchases by corporations, associations, and others. For details, contact the publisher at the address above.

Orders by US trade bookstores and wholesalers: Please contact the publisher at the address above.

Dedicated to Robert Frost,
who inspires me to reach for the title of
Poet

Contents

Author's Note

I think a lot about the circle of life, in part because I'm getting up in years, but also because I'm highly spiritual by nature—more on that in a moment. From a scientific viewpoint, it's pretty straightforward: Organisms are spawned in one way or another, grow to maturity, reproduce, and eventually die. Death is inevitable, but so is the rise of new life to take the place of the departed and begin the circle of life anew.

We humans participate in this grand adventure, of course, but we tend to look beyond the science to make sense of it. There are endless schools of thought here. Many organized religions teach that we have a single go-around and that upon death, our morality (or lack thereof) is judged by a higher power for the purpose of determining an appropriate afterlife. At the other end of the spectrum, nihilists scoff at the notion of morality and contend our appearance on planet Earth holds no meaning whatsoever.

This collection of my poetry is written through an entirely different lens—that of Buddhism and other spiritual paths I have studied over the past 35-plus years. One of the key tenets of all these paths is that each of us travels the circle of life not once but many, many times, taking on a new identity in life after life so we can learn and grow and inch our way up the evolutionary spiral towards enlightenment.

Along the way, we have ample opportunity to experiment with good and evil . . . morality and immorality . . . compassion and cruelty . . . productive and destructive behaviors . . . and to experience the outcome of those experiments in our everyday lives. We take what we learn from one life into the next, and who we are in any given life is a direct reflection of who we have been in all our previous lives. Along the way, we answer for our choices through the workings of karma. Yes—karma really did see that.

This book is an intensely personal undertaking because it is an outgrowth of my journey around the circle in this life, as well as in certain past lives that I am privileged to remember at least in part. A few of the poems also reflect past life memories that others have shared with me. The collection is organized into three groups of poems:

- The first group, *Love Goes On*, comprises poems inspired by certain individuals or groups of people I have been deeply connected with in the past or present;
- The second group, *Spiritual Truths*, addresses key spiritual lessons that have been driven home to me in many lives, including this one; and
- The final group, *Darkening Firmament*, contains poems that bear witness in one way or another to the degeneration of the human experience—and the planet as a whole—that has become evident during my current life.

The title of this book, *Dancing Through Seafoam*, speaks to another aspect of our journey around the circle—the brevity and fragility of life. Sometimes our lives are cut short by disease, accidents, violence, or other events. At any rate, it is trite but true to say that our time goes by in the blink of an eye—like smoke through a keyhole, as the movie *The Bucket List* so famously put it. To me, it seems that life is like a dance through the seafoam that disappears almost as fast as it forms along the seashore. One moment it and you are there—and the next, both are gone.

I sincerely hope my poetry helps you enjoy the dance a little more.

— Diane Skye Gropper
December 2024

Love Goes On

Love is the truth. Love is the light.

— Lama Surya Das

For Michael

You don't know me
in this life.
We haven't met
this time around.

You may not remember me,
but I remember you.
I remember how it was
when we knew each other, then.

I remember your long black hair,
the lines of your body,
the scent of your copper skin,
the soft tones of your voice.

I remember how you looked at me
when you held me,
when you touched me.
Everything stopped in those moments.

I remember how you loved our babies,
how you played with them,
how you sang to them
each night by the fire.

I remember how we laughed together,
how we marveled at the magic
of the dancing blue-green grasses
on the endless high plains.

I remember how I left
when you left.
How I could not find the will
to go on without you.

In all my lives
since beginningless time,
I've known love like that only once—
with you, then.

You don't know me
in this life.
It doesn't matter
because . . . I know you.

After You

I noticed the change
as soon as you left.
I saw it, I felt it,
it was everywhere.
There was a soft sadness,
an air of quiet anguish
that hung like a pall.
There was less light in the world,
less sparkle in the spring sun.

The earth stopped turning,
the birds stopped trilling,
the clock stopped ticking.
My breath grew shallow
with grief.

Life hurried on
but made even less sense than before.
The finely spun fabric of existence was torn
and there was no way to mend it.

I'm sure you had your reasons,
but I wonder—

Didn't you know
what a difference you made?

In Absentia

You are always close, child,
though you are not here
and never were.

A day lily, a shooting star,
a soft caress. None of these
linger and neither did you.

No chance to count your
fingers and toes. Just grief
that stitched my womb shut.

You left as you came, a free
spirit whose visit taught me
that even loss holds a gain.

I often see your dreamlike
form dancing like a gypsy in
the seafoam on Cape Cod.

You twirl to a stop and your
knowing eyes tell me there is
no such thing as absent.

Casablanca

(i)
You know, the truth is,
we really might have missed each other.
It could have gone either way.

Both of us
haunted, always haunted
by the same dreams.
Though we hadn't met,
both of us assuring ourselves
they were just dreams,
when deep inside
we knew they were memories.

(ii)
Memories of riding together
on a small grey burro
with a stubby mane
and stubborn way
of picking her path through
the rocks and ravines
of the desert terrain of Judea,
captured by slavers and
headed to Jerusalem,
where,
in the hellish heat

of the open markets,
we would each be sold
to the highest bidder,
for one purpose or another.

Though you and I had spoken little,
when there was a pause
for the animals to drink,
we looked into each other's eyes
and though no one
had ever told us as much,
that day we learned firsthand
that the eyes are indeed
the window to the soul,
and that a soul,
once recognized,
leaves an imprint on another soul
that is never forgotten.

We hurriedly whispered a plan,
and when night came
and the guards were drunk
from their daily ration of new wine,
we slipped from our ties,
took each other's hand,
and stole away into the dark,
making our way to one village
and then another and another,
heading south, always south,
then following a trading caravan
laden with dates and figs and olives

slowly trundling in that direction,
to the land of our birth.

When we reached that land,
our land,
others, dark like us,
paid scarce attention
to a young man and a young woman
making a life together,
working on small farms
along the Nile,
and then on our own farm,
harvesting barley and pomegranates,
and later blue and white lotuses
that made us a name
and gave us a life of ease.

But the ease never erased
the memory of our journey south,
and with that ever in mind,
gratitude marked our every step
as we raised our crops
and our flowers
and our children,
and as we contemplated
that we owed it all
to a shared ride
on a small grey burro.

And there we stayed
as the sun rose and set,
never leaving each other's side
. . . until we had to.

(iii)
Both of us
haunted, always haunted
by these memories.
Memories of a union
that was forged in peril
but grew into a lifetime
of love and family,
a lifetime of the deepest
devotion, trust and reliance
that two people can know.
Memories of what was,
what could be again,
perhaps.

Both of us
searching, always searching
the eyes of those we met,
looking for the long-lost imprint
of the one we knew so well,
not consciously, of course,
but as a matter of second nature,
driven by some relentless inner force
that could not be calmed,
could not be ignored,
and gave no peace.

And then,
the search came to an end
when we found each other
one cold and rainy
Monday night in October,
seemingly by accident
(is there such a thing?),
when we least expected it,
on the way home from work,
and in the most unlikely place,
by the cookie counter
at a deli on the Upper West Side
that, unbeknownst to us,
we both favored
for take-home dinners.

Our eyes locked
and our breath stopped
for just a moment
as the recognition dawned.
Later, we would share the memories,
but at that moment,
we were stunned
as we stood
face-to-face
with a total stranger
that we each knew,
in every cell,
in every recess of our being,
was anything but.

You leaned close to me.
Of all the gin joints,
you whispered in my ear.
And then you smiled
and took my hand,
and we walked out
into the pouring rain.

No umbrellas.

No Turning Back

"Whereof what's past is prologue;
what to come in yours and my discharge."

– William Shakespeare, The Tempest

A line is crossed.

Something long left unsaid
is said.
The truth crystallizes
into view,
cold and unforgiving.

Nothing is as it was.

Shock careens.
Tempers flare.
Hearts pound.
Minds race—
filled with stupid,
trite thoughts:

The cat's out of the bag.
Our cards are on the table.
Nowhere to run, nowhere to hide.

Both parties paralyzed,
wishing the line hadn't been
crossed.

Fearing
what's past is prologue
to a future that no longer
exists.

Yantacaw

I dream of it. Often.

I walk the familiar path that arcs around the pond,
find a seat on the wooden bench that always beckons
and surrender to the spell of Yantacaw,
letting it ferry me away to parts unknown

like a dream within a dream.

For many, it's just a pleasant park in a bustling
New Jersey town, pretty and peaceful, nothing more.
But for me, it has always been hallowed ground,
a sanctuary that absolves the madness of the world,
a balm for my aching spirit, a portal to the inner stillness

I often seek yet rarely find.

I see them in my dreams, the ghosts of the Yantacaw
natives who once called this place home, who grew maize
and beans and squash and fished the teeming waters and
hunted the dense, mossed woods for deer and bear.
Today, their lands are occupied by parkways and Circle Ks
and houses, so many houses, but I see them still because

Yantacaw goes on.

Now, as then, stately elms, sycamores, and oaks stand
like guardians, offering refuge from the sun, while red

maples splash the landscape with color and weeping willows charm with their untamed shapes. The pristine egret stands on one leg by the pond's edge and then powerfully leaps aloft to circle like a white marble angel

carved by Michelangelo himself.

At the heart of the pond, a fountain sends spray to the Gods and the droplets prism the sunlight into rainbow pinpoints before falling back to begin again. The elusive wood turtle pops its head above the surface to sun on a rock, while a blue dragonfly skims the surface and then darts in my direction and alights on the back of my bench

to grace me with its magic.

A scarlet blur races around the edge of the pond so quickly I can barely make out the bushy tail of a red fox, while a doe and her fawn sip water from the creek that feeds the pond and the yellow trout lilies dotting the ground sloping up from the water sway in a faint breeze. Yantacaw's flora and fauna make me

catch my breath with awe.

I now live far from Yantacaw, but it is never far from me in my dream or waking moments, always calling to me, always reminding me of where my real home lies, like a compass shows true north. I heed its siren call and in my final moments, I shall know that

Yantacaw awaits me.

Adonai

carbon bits where once was breath
bear witness to a conflagration
like an archeological find
of a crematorium

depravity descended
smearing pestilence in its unholy wake
shrieking with delight at its fleeting victory
and caring not
that it only deepens the stain on its pocked face
because depravity never learns

blackened vestiges
of chairs and clothes
coffee mugs and photos
rattles and teddy bears
bedding and rugs heavy with blood
shards of DNA ruthlessly rendered
from the corpus animus of your people
waft in the light of dawn
mocking its promise

never again we said
but again rose from the ground
like a venomous geyser
scalding us with the magma of malevolence

we know so well
a universal witch's brew
that has smoldered and seethed
for eternity

we could ask why
but we know better
because we've had to ask it too many times before
we know only
that this is what you've chosen us for

we are charred and gouged
and marred by grief
but like the burning bush
we are not consumed
and we will not go gentle into the night
we will burn and rave
we will rage, rage
and never allow
the dying of our light*

---

* *The author acknowledges the inspiration and words of Dylan Thomas in the last verse of this poem. See his poem Do Not Go Gentle Into That Good Night.*

Rinpoche

The old man was wakened by the clatter of a tin cup hitting the rock floor of the cave. The embers in his fire still glowed but did little to stop the winter air of the high Himalayas from scratching at him with its steel claws.

> The intruder, a mere lad, stopped short, silently kicking himself for the misstep that had tumbled the cup and announced his presence.

Who's there, asked the old man as he slowly rose up on his straw mat and tightened his tattered cloak about his bony shoulders. His voice betrayed no fear because he felt none.

> I'm a thief! shouted the boy, trying to sound frightful. I've come to steal your valuables!

My valuables, chuckled the old man. Would you call the cup you just knocked to the ground a valuable? Or how about the basket of dried yak dung I keep to stoke the fire? There's nothing of value here and nothing to compare with the finery you could find in the wealthy homes of the village at the foot of the mountain.

What made you climb the mountain to visit the abode of an old Buddhist monk?

> The boy hesitated. The monks at the monastery in the village, they told me...they told me, he stammered...

Don't be afraid, said the old man as he rose to fetch some dung. You are shivering—come, have a seat by the fire, warm yourself and tell me what they said.

> The boy sat down cross-legged near the growing fire. I often help the monks in the fields behind the monastery, he said quietly, and they told me you know how to find jewels that are worth more than all the riches of all the wealthy people everywhere. My family is poor, we have so little to eat, so I came to steal a jewel from you. As he finished, he turned his head away in shame.

The old man studied the boy for a long time before answering. I have good news for you, my son, he finally said. You've no need to steal a jewel from me because you already have one.

> The boy sat stunned for a moment and then jumped to his feet to wildly search his pockets. When he found nothing, his face fell. You make light of me, he whispered. I have no such treasure. If I did, I'd know it.

Well, you see, that's the problem, said the old man. You do possess this treasure, we all do. But we don't know it because it's not the kind of jewel we can see and touch and hold up to sparkle in the sun. It is a hidden jewel buried deep within us, in the essence we carry from life to life.

The boy looked baffled. What good is *that* kind of jewel, he asked.

What the monks in the village told you is true, replied the old man. The jewel within is worth more than all the riches of all the wealthy people in the world. It is our true nature, our Buddha nature, and only this true nature can rescue us from the suffering we experience in life after life. You are young, but I'm sure you've already witnessed the bitterness of human suffering.

The boy gazed into the fire for a long time and then spoke quietly. My village is all I know, but I have seen much suffering there. Many villagers work hard but have so little that they often go cold and hungry. A flood killed some of the crops during the rains last spring, making things worse. My father often falls ill, and my mother cries every night because my baby sister died suddenly a few months ago—why, we do not know. And not just the poor suffer. Last year, one of the richest men in the village lost his home and many of his animals to a fire, and then his wife

ran off with another man, leaving him to care
for all their children. Yes, I have seen suffering.

The old man's heart hurt as he listened to the boy recount these tales of misery, grief and loss. It is called samsara, he said when the boy had finished. All of us are locked in an endless cycle of rebirth, suffering and death. The only way to break the iron chains of samsara is to find the jewel within and become that jewel—the Buddha we truly are.

How do you find the jewel? asked the boy.

By following the teachings of Buddha and the other enlightened masters, said the old man. It takes years of study and meditation to strip away the dirt covering the jewel—the delusions, bad karma and negative patterns. More likely, lifetimes of work. It is a difficult road but the highest calling you can follow.

And your jewel . . . have you uncovered it? the
boy asked hesitantly.

Not yet, the old man replied slowly. But every day, I rededicate myself to the task. Buddha teaches that you must never lose hope because you never know how close you are to finding it.

There's something I don't understand, said the boy. How does finding your jewel do away with suffering?

My son, said the old man while shaking his head. That is something that I could not explain to you in one sitting or even 100. Only years of study bring that wisdom to you.

I want to find my jewel! exclaimed the boy.

The old man smiled knowingly. I believe that is the real reason you climbed the mountain to find me, he said. You thought you were looking for one type of jewel but were really seeking another.

If I come to see you every week, will you teach me the path to follow? implored the boy.

The old man sat silent for a few moments. I long ago stopped teaching so that I could devote myself to solitary meditation and study in my cave. But I will take you on as a student because I can see how sincere you are. If you like, I can give you your first teaching today. I will make some butter tea and we can begin.

Wait, said the boy. I don't even know your name. What shall I call you?

What would you like to call me, asked the old man.

> The monks in the village told me you are so wise that I should honor you by addressing you as Precious One, or Rinpoche, said the boy. That is what I'd like to call you.

Then Rinpoche it is, said the old man. And he began brewing the butter tea.

Pax Romana

Good fences make good neighbors,
    [a great poet once wrote.]
Not so for you and I.

Our fences are good
    [—too good—]
so stoutly constructed of concrete
and asphalt and the fallacy we are
strangers that they keep us far apart
and far away from the unfinished
business between us.

What that may be is hard to say but
    [our souls know]
because that's what propelled you to
trek across a continent and settle into
a sand-colored house with a red tile
roof and concrete block fence on the
other side of the street from my sand-
colored house with a red tile roof
and concrete block fence. 2,000 miles
crumbled to 200 feet and there we
were, eye to eye across a ribbon
of blacktop.

Your appearance onstage was
[no random event,]
however tempting it may be to paint
it that way, and to call it such is to
dishonor the exquisite mosaics our
paths follow in life after life—an
astonishing sequence of spiritual
designs powered by free will, flush
with opportunity and assembled by
our highest selves and that Great
Enabler, the Universe, to help us
inch our way, rung by rung, up the
evolutionary spiral.

We are strangers in this life, yes, but
[not really strangers]
because you and I have walked side
by side before. That much I knew the
moment I saw you and since then
my dreams have paraded snatches of
of an ancient life of ours marked
by tragic turns that the Bard himself
might have penned. Betrothed as
youths, I betrayed you by running
away with another, but you never
stopped loving me and stood by me
when he left me and the son he had
fathered to marry into wealth. My
folly robbed us of what could have
been and in the end we were both

scorned by our own unforgiving
community.

Grief scarred that life
    [like acid rain]
and remnants of it run to this day
through the rivers of our souls. Now
our mosaics have brought our rivers
close again, allowing us a chance to
cleanse our waters so we can both
move on a little easier, a little
lighter. Will we squander this gift or
use it to heal? We need not be family
or lovers or even close friends.
Perhaps it's enough to just be good
neighbors—despite the fences.

For my part, I seek a lasting peace,
    [a Pax Romana,]
for our spirits. So let these words be
my peace offering and may this poem
be my emissary.

It's your move.

Sierra Madre

Good things come in small packages,
I often told my mother. I towered over
her and called her shrimp. She laughed
and told me I had gotten my big bones

and height from my father. I was her
youngest and we were indelibly bonded
because she was my savior and I was
hers in a family haunted by madness

and strife. She stroked my hair when I
kneeled and put my head in her lap as
she sat at the sparkly Formica table in
the kitchen, drinking her ever-present

black coffee and smoking her menthol
cigarettes and recounting the latest
gossip her friend next door had shared
that day. She was the bedrock, the

tectonic footing of that household and
its sole beacon of love. Yet she was
invisible to everyone but me, like a door
or a car or a teapot you need and depend

on every day but don't really see or even
acknowledge, much less appreciate.
Grace is bestowed only upon those with
open hearts. I did my best to show her

how much she mattered to me and saved
my pennies each week to buy her a
carnation from the local florist. Pink and
white were her favorites but no matter

what color I brought home, she beamed
and proudly put the flower in a special
vase reserved for this little ritual of ours.
I did my best but in the end it was not

enough and she slipped away far, far too
early. After that, I was long lost, adrift in
a miasma of anguish. What saved me
were the tectonics she had instilled in me–

the mettle to live against the grain, the
passion to mine for the truth, the abiding
resolve to never become a prisoner, not
even of those I love. These singular gifts

empowered me to dream in an unorthodox
but wholly authentic and magickal life.
With joy, I now see my daughter etching
out her own authentic arc, a gift less from

me than from the grandmother she never
knew. Even now, I sometimes still buy a
carnation for my mother and put it in a
special vase reserved for this ritual. I have

no idea where she is right now—what life
or planet or dimension she is traversing.
But I know she knows how things turned
out and I am quite certain she is beaming.

Surrender

"We loved with a love that was
more than love."

–Edgar Allan Poe, Annabel Lee

There's something in the stars
that brings us together yet holds us apart.
Not quite star-crossed lovers,
but close.

Bound by a love so profound, so sacred,
it brings us to our knees.
Bound by a connection of our souls
forged an eternity ago.

But separated, always separated,
by the stark realities of our divergent worlds.
Worlds that cannot hope to find
common ground.

We choose to accept the separation,
this rending of our love,
in an act of surrender.

We choose to let go of the thought
that things should be anything other
than exactly what they are.

We choose surrender over the
unfathomable alternative.

The Falconer

I laughed the first time he said it
one beautiful, early summer morning.
I laughed because it sounded so odd.
But what did I know? I was only fifteen.

Watch for the falcon! he yelled in a
mock British accent, pointing to the sky.
What do you mean by that? I asked.
He did not reply, but his eyes were smiling.
He was enjoying the moment
and he said it again.

Watch for the falcon.
Watch for the falcon.

I am sure he did not know why he said
those words or ascribe much meaning to them.
My father was given to saying strange things.
He was different that way, eccentric.
But even then, as young as I was,
I knew deep inside these words held meaning.
I would puzzle over them for years to come
and vowed to never forget them.

I tried to tell him how I felt,
but we could never really talk about anything.

You see, words were hard to come by between us
and he was harsh on those he loved.
And so I—
I could not change him and us.
I could not bridge the missed connection.
But what did I know? I was only fifteen.

All that summer, as he traveled the country,
he sent me postcards from his journey.
They all ended with the same words:
Watch for the falcon. I could hear him
yelling them in his silly British accent.
I could see him pointing to the sky.
I could feel his eyes smiling.

After that summer, he never spoke of
this again, not even when I asked him to.
But I saved all his postcards and
have them to this day.

Years went by and he left this life.
I felt despair when he died and mourned
our missed connection. I often read the
saved postcards, but their meaning remained
out of reach. Then, when I was in my fifties,
about the age he had been that summer,
I went on a journey of my own—
a physical and spiritual one.

Along the way, I learned of a life I had
long ago in England, living on an estate

owned by an aristocrat who had a passion
for hunting. His hunts were known
as the finest in the land in no small measure
because I was his falconer.
The best, he often said, he had ever known.

M' lord was a learned man, a good man,
demanding, but kind to all he knew.
He treated me more as a son than a servant
and gave me a home throughout that life.
It was he who had me trained in falconry.
When I took to it beyond all expectation,
he made me his head falconer at a young age
and told me I was born to the craft.

For years, I led his hunting parties.
His anticipation grew when I released the falcon,
knowing it would lead us to prey,
his excitement carried him away.
Watch for the falcon! he exclaimed,
pointing to the sky, his eyes smiling.
Watch for the falcon!

Lifetimes later, these memories were gifted to me
by some unknown force as an act of healing.
A precious link between two lives,
between two fathers who were one in the same.
At last, the long-held mystery was solved,
the meaning of the words laid bare.
I cried in awe and gratitude
at the beauty of the revelation.

What made my father utter those words
that beautiful early summer morning?
Decades later, his youngest child
finally had an answer.
He, too, sensed our missed connection.
It pained him, even I could see.
Despite being older and wiser,
he could no more heal it than could I.
Out of the depths of his very being,
from the deepest reservoir of memories,
came the words that his soul knew
would one day reconnect us.

Those words have taught me a profound lesson
about the dance we do from life to life,
connecting with souls again and again
as we walk the path of evolution.
I now know those connections are never lost.
They may ebb or flow in some lives,
but the golden strands that bind us
forever hold us close.

Since then, I've never looked back.
I've ceased mourning what couldn't be.
Healed by the truth he taught me—
that the bonds of the soul endure.

As I near the end of this life,
I take great comfort from that wisdom.
We will connect again, if not next time,
then another. I sometimes reach out

to tell him I'll see him again.
But he already knows that
and his eyes are smiling.

Until then, I wish him Godspeed
in the best way I know how.
Watch for the falcon,
I tell my beloved father.
Watch for the falcon.

Spiritual Truths

Live as if you were to die tomorrow.
Learn as if you were to live forever.

— Mahatma Gandhi

Bling

Fortune and fame.
Flashing paparazzi lights.
Drinks on the house.
Raucous Talladega nights.

Big wads of cash
to buy your own plane.
Botox and face lifts
to comfort the vain.

Sex, drugs and booze,
lots of distractions.
Bet your favorite sport,
get in on the action.

Power in the boardroom.
Muscle in the market.
Hobnob with celebrities.
Strut the red carpet.

Fancy cars and big houses.
High-end vacations.
Destination weddings.
Impressive vocations.

Keep up with the Joneses.
Marry that trophy wife.
Buy everything that's trendy.
Live the good life.

So where does all this get us?
Does it change a damn thing?
In the end, what's the value
of all this shiny bling?

Deep down you know the truth,
that it's empty as can be.
That it only takes you away
from what can truly set you free.

You can choose to take the red pill
or (like so many) you can choose to take the blue.
Just remember—everything rides
on what you choose to do.

So go ahead…

Binge-watch TV.
Drink another beer.
Anything to forget
why you're really here.

Samsara, o samsara,
your bling binds us and blinds us
to the price we pay
day after day.

Life after life.

To An Old Friend

"Death is always smiling at us.
All we can do is smile back."

– Marcus Aurelius*

I feel bad for you, old friend.
No one understands you.
  Or is it that no one chooses to?

You always smile at us,
not to intimidate, but to bring to mind
  what we want to forget.

You remind us of the truth of this life,
the truth that you ensure.
  Time is short, tick tock.

It's tempting to ignore that truth,
to live like tomorrow's endless.
  But that's the ultimate folly.

You urge us to get real each morning,
to openly admit that
  today could be the day.

Only then can we muster the clarity
to wisely use our greatest gift—
    whatever time is left.

You've come to us over the aeons
in one life after another,
    prodding us to get it.

But we prefer to blithely meander,
missing the opportunity each life affords.
    We live deaf, dumb and blind.

Like the devoted friend you are,
you never give up on us.
    You smile with inexhaustible patience.

You wait for us to reach the Pure Land
when we will need you no more.
    But then your time, too, will be done.

So in the end, old friend,
perhaps we should ask:
    Who's smiling at who?

** This quote is often attributed to Marcus Aurelius, Roman emperor (161 – 180 AD) and Stoic philosopher, though not all historians agree he actually said it.*

Requiem for an Assassin

I never saw it coming,
that rope you slipped around my neck,
glinting like steel,
so silvery and thin like an assassin's garotte.
Oh, I noticed you idly fingering it when we met,
as it dangled from your belt loop,
but I never imagined you would reach for it,
like a gun in a gunfight,
a weapon of choice,
a means of annihilation.

Keep your friends close and your enemies closer,
a famous gangster once said.
Keep your enemies cloaked as friends the closest,
I have learned.

You caught me by surprise only briefly
because I've met your kind before—
so common as to almost be trite,
yet somehow surprising with each meeting
for those more trusting in nature.
Ostentatious spiritual migrators
who peddle unctuous smiles to your face
and noxious schemes behind your back,
who bill themselves as savants
and crow about their devotion to the path

but miscarry in living its teachings,
who throw out well-rehearsed tidbits
like bread and circus to win the crowd,
building alliances in dark whispers,
mouthing fables and twisted wisps of truth
that sweep even the innocent-minded
into their snares.

Time has taught me that your kind
wanders the earth like hungry ghosts,
hollowed-out stumps in human form,
with blackened innards that the
external frock of piety cannot shield
from those given to seeing the truth.

We could have coexisted,
imperfect travelers side-by-side,
but you could not bear
my lack of devotion to you,
and the assassin's cloak suits you well.
So you bided your time and made your move,
and your satisfaction waxed
as the rope fell into place
atop my shoulders.

Ah, the best laid plans of mice and men,
we all know what can happen to them.
Imagine your surprise
when the rope proved little more than you,
decayed and brittle,
vacant at its core,

a mere puff of smoke
as I sloughed it off
and veered away unscathed.

I wasn't your first
and surely won't be your last.
But I rejoice not
in your hollow heart,
because I know it will assassinate

only you.

Boomerang

I woke up one night
and there he was,
standing by my bed.
Buddha.
The one and only
Shakyamuni,
illuminated by the
multicolored lights
of my Target alarm clock.
Red, blue, green, yellow, white
rays of light streaming around him,
coruscating and filling
the whole of my bedroom
with the wisdom colors
of the Universe.

He looked younger
than I might have imagined,
far too young to be Enlightened,
and rather ordinary,
like the Everyman
you pass without notice
on the street.
But Buddha he was,
I knew in my heart,
and though I was stunned

to be in his presence,
I found him
strangely calming.

Buddha, I whispered
as I bowed my head,
I am honored to meet you,
but I must ask:
Why are you here?

He gazed at me
and smiled gently.
Perhaps I should ask you
the same question,
he replied.

Thwack!
His answer hit me like a boomerang,
since I had asked myself
that question so many times.
Years and years and years
of living the spiritual seeker's life,
questing for answers to the
great questions of existence,
pursuing them with
strategic care and diligence
like a hunter stalks big game.
Devouring sacred texts,
madly scribbling notes
at countless teachings,
shutting myself away at retreats,

praying like my life depended on it,
and meditating
for days, weeks, months,
lifetimes, it sometimes seemed,
sitting cross-legged and stiff-backed
until my body screamed *no more!*
and my mind sought relief
in binge-watching
mindless sitcoms on TV.
Straining for the slightest clue
to the nature and location of Nirvana,
desperately wishing
I could set an inner GPS
to get me there,
tormented by stabs of doubt
(am I making any progress?)
and at my worst moments
wondering . . .does it even exist?
. . . or am I just a parched traveler
dragging myself across hot sands
toward an oasis that is
but a mirage.

So here I was,
in the presence of the Master.
Cut to the chase, I thought.
It's not as if he doesn't know
where you stand.

Buddha, I said.
I am a devoted seeker.

But do you know
how many lifetimes
it will take me
to reach Enlightenment
if I keep going at this pace?

Do you know
how many it will take
if you don't?
he swiftly replied.

With that, he softly touched
the crown of my head
and receded into
the darkness of the night,
leaving the radiance
of my alarm clock
to illuminate my path ahead.

I drifted to sleep
on the current of his blessings
and dreamed
I became a Buddha.

Dimensions

In the world we inhabit,
that tiresome reality
we call home,
dimensions
limit possibilities.

The trinity of 3D-ism,
length/height/width
measured oh-so-carefully,
calls the shots on
what fits, what doesn't.
Time, the ruler of our lives,
is singular.
Seconds/minutes/hours
run only one way,
forward.

In the worlds
we do not inhabit,
the ones we cannot
see or feel
but which exist
nonetheless,
defying imagination,
dimensions
create possibilities.

These worlds
are dimensions.
Diverse dimensions
of existence,
multiverses
layered one upon another
and another,
interconnected and
too numerous to count,
stacked and interwoven,
like strands in a fabric,
spanning multiple
planets, universes and
planes of actuality,
a cacophony of colors
vibrations and dreamscapes,
parallel realities teeming
with life of every kind,
human and not,
corporeal and not,
fathomable and not,
including lives we
have had or may have,
or are having right now,
even as we live this one,
and streams of consciousness
of all manner of beings.

Time is fluid
in these dimensions,
running forward, backward,

concurrent.
Time as we know it
does not exist.

Sometimes,
when it's least expected,
the world we inhabit
touches those we do not
through portals that
open and close
for reasons unknown,
piercing the shrouded
veils between them,
and life reaches out to life
across dimensions,
inviting connection
between it and us,
between form and nonform,
between form and
forms unknown.

Who's to say
we shouldn't
accept that invitation?
Isn't that why we're here?
Not just to be born
and grow up
and go to work
and pay bills
and raise kids
and get old and die,

but to take risks and
grow the spirit
by any means possible.
Who's to say
we won't find
magic in the connection?
Or even love,
the longing of all life?

Life reaches out to life
across dimensions.
Who's to say?

Cholla

Inspired by Robert Frost's "Dust of Snow"

The prick of the cholla
here and there
brings to mind the pain
I'd rather not bear.

And spurs me ahead
in my ongoing search
for a balm to release
the memories of hurt.

I thank the cholla
for the blood it has drawn
as I lighten my load
and smiling, move on.

Clueless

it's a double-edged sword
the free will we possess

exhilarating
terrifying
emancipating
enslaving
blessing
curse
asset
albatross
best friend
worst enemy

gifted to us by the gods
free will is
the driver of our choices
the motor that propels us
always at our beck and call
to put to use as the
Commanders-in-Chief
of our lives
for better or naught
but at its best enabling us
to boldly go
where we've never gone before

to broaden the ambit
of our endeavors
to spiritually soar
like the majestic beings
we are meant to be

but here's the reality

much of the time
we stumble about
like clueless morons
unmindful
of the power of this gift
unmindful
of the downside of this gift
unmindful
we even possess this gift
along the way bringing little
conscious thought
or higher wisdom
or checks on our basest instincts
to our decision making

instead we take
a fistful of jealousy
and add it to
a pound of prejudice
and a ton of ignorance
to whip up the
choices we make

and the actions we take
in our everyday lives

and then we wonder why
the world is disfigured
and disintegrating

we wonder why
we're not where we wanted to go
and who we wanted to be

we wonder why
we feel vacant and ill-fated

we scratch our heads
and ask ourselves
what's wrong with this picture
or worse yet
don't even recognize
how wrong the picture really is

we defeat ourselves
with the very sword
that could set us free

it would be funny
were it not so tragic

If You Knew

If you knew
absolutely everything matters . . .

Even if you don't believe that,
let's say, for just one moment,
you *knew* it to be true.

If you knew
your thoughts you believe are so private, count,
your words you can't take back, count,
your actions, miniscule or momentous, count.

If you knew
who you were in your past lives
shaped who you are in this one,
and who you choose to be in this one
will shape who you are in countless lives to come.

If you knew
the best and worst of you,
the good, the bad and the ugly,
will be yours forever more—

The lies you casually spin,
the honesty you strive for,
the evil thoughts you entertain,

the virtuous beliefs you live by,
the hate you spew online,
the love you feel for your family,
the harsh judgments you rush to make,
the compassion you show for others,
the greed that makes you crave more,
the gratitude that says you have enough,
the intolerance that clouds your thinking,
the open-mindedness you embrace,
the jealousy that poisons your heart,
the joy you find in helping others succeed,
the indifference you show to cruelty,
the premium you place on being kind,
the spiritual void you feel inside,
the abiding faith you hold in the above.

If you knew
all those things
and all others
plant karmic seeds in your soul
that carry forward,
from one life to the next,
and that those seeds may lay fallow
for no time or a long time,
maybe even for lifetimes,
but that they inevitably ripen
bringing the essence
of your vast past history
of thoughts, words and actions
back to you.

Maybe your karma
will bring you
health, wealth and happiness.
Maybe it will bring you
disease, poverty and misery.
Or maybe it will bring you
something in between.
But whatever it brings
reflects the sum total
of who you were before
and whatever comes your way
is inescapable.

Not as punishment
or retribution
or payback.
But due to cause and effect.
Every element of cause
has an inevitable effect.
It's really pretty simple,
a basic scientific law
we all know and understand
because we see it in action
every day, all around us.

When you kick a ball,
it rolls away.
When you drop a glass,
it shatters.
And on and on.
So why is it surprising

that what you think, say and do
holds consequence for you?
Perhaps not today, but some day.

Unlike the ball
and the glass,
we have a choice
at every moment.
We can shape what lies ahead
by rewriting our script
of cause and effect,
by consciously choosing
our thoughts, words and deeds.
Or we can play dumb
to the laws of the Universe
and roll the dice.

If you knew
you could transform everything,
not just in this life
and your future lives
but in the lives of others
and the whole of existence
by consciously writing your script
of cause and effect.

Even if you don't believe that,
let's say, for just one moment,
you *knew* it to be true.
If you knew
what would you do

Different?

Quandary

Such a quandary
for those of us accustomed to living by the brain.
For someone like me whose lifelong motto has been:
When in doubt, fall back on logic.

Logic—
The foot soldier of the brain. The ultimate arbiter of
analytics. Driven by facts, figures, research, evidence.
Dot every i, cross every t, assess every risk. All this
to build a bunker of unassailable truth to avoid peril
at all costs. Don't start that business. Don't fall in love.
Don't take chances.

Safe. Secure. Reliable. And a prison.
A prison that locks out the heart,
that which above all else makes us human.

The heart—
The spokesperson of the soul's yearning. The gateway
to creativity, leaps of faith and vision. The portal to
passion and love. The heart prods us to reach for what
we really want—climb that mountain, write that poem,
strive for Enlightenment. It fuels our imagination, our
will to right wrongs, our search for a mate to meld with
at day's end.

Be wary of the heart, says the brain.
It could make a fool of you.

Be wary of the brain, says the heart.
Live by the sword, die by the sword.

Such a quandary for those of us accustomed to living by the sword, someone like me. Longing to back away from the brain, to stop playing it safe, to let my heart take charge, but petrified of what might happen if I leave the bunker of logic. I could stumble and fall, utterly fail, or watch my heart get shattered.

I'm on the cusp, teetering…but I trust what my instinct tells me. The sword can only take me so far. Logic has its limits so why not admit I'm already treading the edge and learn to walk it with courage.

Quandary no more. Heart, lead the way!

Epiphany

What could have been.
Would have been.
Should have been.

I deserved better.
I took a wrong turn.
I caught a bad break.

I'm down on my luck.
It's me against the world.
I just can't win.

It's his fault.
It's her fault.
It's their fault.

She wronged me.
He misled me.
They cheated me.

Why doesn't she like me?
Why doesn't he love me?
Why don't they accept me?

It's not fair.
It's not right.
Life sucks.

Stop.

Do you believe your life is random?
Are you that out of touch?
Do you really think what happens to you
is just a matter of luck?

What if all that comes your way
is supposed to be there
and has absolutely nothing to do
with what's right or just or fair.

Suppose that all your ebbs and flows
are of your own karmic making,
designed to help you learn and grow,
a lesson for the taking.

Just imagine how freeing it would be
to swear off being blind,
to accept the fact that you're in charge
and leave self-pity behind.

So if you really want to change course
and bring Enlightenment nearer,
stop indulging in the blame game
and take a look in the mirror.

Memento Mori

"When it comes your time to die . . . sing your death song and die like a hero going home."

– Tecumseh, Shawnee Warrior Chief

They say how you die
is just as important as how you live.
Whoever they are, they're right.

What will my *how* be like this time,
I sometimes muse.

Will I die with strength and honor
like I did when I was a Roman legionnaire,
determined to give all until my last moment
to gain entrance to the Fields of Elysium,
the final resting place of those blessed
by the gods. I'll see your head on a stick,
I growled at the barbarian charging me
in Germania and as his knife pierced my
heart, I summoned the will to gouge out
his eyes with my bare hands and saw
Elysium beckoning as I floated away
from my lifeless form.

Will I stand tall in the face of death
like I did when I was an Apache chief,
choosing to meet death as an equal,
to depart on my terms so I could die the
good death all warriors seek. Surrounded
by the Mexican army in northern Chihuahua,
outnumbered and watching my men die,
I took my knife and slit myself open from
groin to heart so I could not be taken alive.
I spat on the Mexicans and laughed at the
disbelief on their faces as I rode my spirit
horse back to the homeland of all Chihenne
at Ojo Caliente.

Will I die with a mind of tranquility
like I was trained to do in countless Buddhist
lives, hoping to secure a higher rebirth. As an
ancient monk at a monastery near Lhasa,
where I had lived since my earliest years, I
could barely draw breath in my final hours.
But inside I found refuge in the clear light of
Mount Meru standing like a beacon at the
center of the Universe and through sheer
strength of mind steered my way through
the bardos on a course to the Pure Land.

Will I remember what I did then when my
time comes again?

Each life brings a renewed challenge of
choices when death comes collecting. We can

succumb to the fear, the pain, the chaos, the regrets. We can fall prey to the aversion all life has to mortality. We can rail about the injustice of a heart gone still.

Or we can choose to depart with strength and honor, however we define it, to meet death as an equal, to bathe in tranquility, to die like a hero going home.

We've done this more than enough times to know that death is but a threshold, and that how we cross it says everything about who we are—and are not.

Memento mori. Remember you will die.
What's your death song?

Internalities

What makes one place home and another not?

It's not about geography, the latitude and longitude, the GPS coordinates, the pin on the map that shows where you were born or grew up or where your family still lives because many of us long from our earliest days to escape those locales.

It's not about where you happen to settle down to take a job or go to school or make your spouse happy, because happenstance is just that.

And it's not about longevity, because God only knows you can live in a place ad nauseum yet forget it once you leave before you hit the edge of town.

No, home is less about externalities than internalities.

Home is where you 100% know you belong based on some undeniable inner truth. It's where you long to go to heal when the undertow of the human condition leaves you wounded. It's where you'd most like to live—if you don't already—and most like to die.

Maybe it's a penthouse in a blaring city. Or a center-hall colonial in a suburban oasis. Or a family farm, a ranch in the desert, a cabin in the woods, a bungalow on the beach, a sailboat on the open ocean.

Wherever and whatever it is, home is your safe harbor where your moorings are secure and everything feels not perfect, but right.

But even that's not the whole story, because there's another kind of home that's not a place or a dwelling but an internality only: the quiet mind that lies deep within, buried beneath the jungle of thoughts we entertain every day but there every moment, offering stillness and refuge.

Beat a retreat to that sacred place and you'll hear the truth that only your soul can speak: *That today's degenerate world is nothing more than a bad movie on a big screen TV…that if you find the wherewith to change for the better, it will, too…and that the key to change is self-love, the rarest of commodities in the wayward human race.*

"The quieter you become, the more you will hear," said Rumi, and the more you hear, the more you will know that your most treasured home is within.

So the next time you want to head home, don't jump in your car or rush to buy a plane ticket. Just take a moment to remind yourself that home is *you.*

The Forest of Zen

Inspired by the verses and koans of Zen Buddhism

Words mean nothing
yet convey all things.

Each of us is a jewel
mired in dirt.

We see time pass
but not our lives.

The bitter melon teaches
more than the sweet.

The fool looks elsewhere
for the treasures at home.

A mind can blind you
more than the eye.

Night and day chase
each other eternally.

Shadows sweep the cat
without ruffling her fur.

The saguaro pricks you
only if you touch it.

Gold has no value when
it is dust in the eye.

All is empty.
Not nonsense. Truth.

Base Camp

"So often times it happens that we live our lives in chains, and we never even know we have the key."

– The Eagles, Already Gone*

I was born in the Base Camp
nestled at the foot of the Mountain.

At night, around the fire, the wise ones told
stories of those who had scaled the Mountain
and the rewards they reaped in doing so.
Few have the strength for the ascent, but
the Clear Light at the summit, they said, will
free you from the chains of human suffering.

At an early age, I knew I had a calling.
My inner voice told me so,
but my inner eyes had not yet opened.
Try as I might, my calling eluded me.
Sometimes I turned to the Mountain for guidance,
but thick clouds shrouded it from view.

As I grew older,
my inner eyes began to open.
Rays of sun pierced the cloud cover.
For the first time, the Mountain came into view.

For the first time—
I knew *it* was my calling.

I wasn't afraid to try,
but I didn't know how to scale the Mountain.
So many paths wound up its sides.
I wasn't sure which path could be relied upon
to guide me to the summit.
I wasn't sure which path was mine.

I tried different paths,
some that I had relied upon in other lives,
others that were brand new.
I began making headway in the climb,
but always lost my footing
and tumbled back to the Base Camp.

As time passed, I lost hope.
I let the false voices take over,
the ones that told me my calling was a pipedream
and that I didn't deserve it anyway.
The ones that said the top could not be scaled
because the Mountain didn't even exist.

For years, those voices gripped me.
I turned my back on the Mountain
and left the Base Camp.
I lived a normal life,
an empty life,
like all lives away from the Mountain.

At night, the Mountain whispered in my ear,
assuring me all was not lost,
urging me to come back.
The false voices faded.
My sense of calling returned.
I left everything to go home.

As I stood before the Mountain,
I saw I didn't have to rely on just one path.
I could follow several paths up,
or better yet,
forge my own path.
The Mountain approved.

Since then, I've never stopped climbing.
Some years, I take my time,
contemplating the view from new heights.
Other years, I speed ahead,
driven by the urgency of time.
But I'm always on the move.

I won't lie, it hasn't been easy.
The ascent has required a revolution within
that has often been unwelcome
as I've shed my skin again and again,
peeling away my self-myths
to reveal who I really am.

There have been times I truly wished
the Mountain was not my calling.
But it is and the wise ones were right:

The climb invests us with the wisdom and will
to pierce the veils of our delusions
and melt away our shackles of ignorance.

My journey is far from over.
The summit still looms well above.
Will I reach it in this life?
Does it matter?
The Clear Light beckons,
assuring me I will reach it in good time.

Below, I can still see the Base Camp
where my story began,
to which I owe everything.
Had I not been born there,
I don't know where I'd be today.
I wave farewell as it grows smaller.

I was born in the Base Camp
nestled at the foot of the Mountain.

One day, I will die at the summit,
bathed in the radiance of the Clear Light.

Emaho.

---

* *"Already Gone," the opening track on the Eagles 1974 album, On the Border, was written by Jack Tempchin and Robb Strandlund.*

Darkening Firmament

Three things cannot be long hidden:
The Sun, the Moon, and the Truth.

— Shakyamuni Buddha

Aperture

Truth is truth.
Or is it?
Depends on if the eyes are
open or shut.
Shut tips the scales to the dark side.
The hell beings
slither out of their dung-filled abodes,
where they eternally lurk
with red eyes and slashing teeth,
waiting for a chance to
poison the truth.
Deceit and denial wipe away
the treachery, treason,
savagery and atrocity
like a Mr. Clean magic eraser.
"Heroes" tweet their minions,
and the shut-eyes nod in unison
for their own corrupt reasons,
like a Greek chorus breaking bad.
Public relations trumps truth
while the godless run rampant,
seeking to vanquish the light
that is our birthright.

Long ago,
a small child in a fairy tale cried out,
"The Emperor has no clothes."
The child has been slain.

Psalm of Serenity

Serenity now! Serenity now! screamed Frank Costanza on a famous episode of Seinfeld. A distinctly un-serene man seeking solace from the madding world.

We laugh, but aren't we all like him?

God grant me the serenity to accept what I cannot change . . . so begins the well-known serenity prayer that appears at every turn. On plaques and posters, t-shirts and t-towels, magnets and mugs, key chains and candles sold on Amazon. Taped to refrigerators at home and computers at work. Eulogized in church sermons and recited feverishly by those in recovery—and those not.

But what of serenity itself, the object of that ubiquitous prayer? Water, water everywhere, but not a drop to drink. We seek serenity, but do we feel it? Or is our search derailed by the dystopic pall that hangs over our current existence?

Where is the serenity in a world where common ground is all but gone and the unhinged run rampant. Where lies are so lionized that truth barely survives. Where hatred taints the air and atrocity is celebrated. Where ecosystems are imploding and microplastics are invading our cells. Where madmen strut forth to become kings flanked by legions of the blind. Where the perennial angst of human existence has metastasized into a cancer on the spirit.

I lie awake some nights watching the ceiling fan turn and wonder if serenity has gone extinct in such a world. But the wiser part of me knows it is alive and well and can be found where it has always lived.

In the surge of our heartbeats and catch between our breaths,
in the stillness of meditation and prayer,
in our gratitude for what we have—and don't have,
in those rare moments we know everything is as it should be,
in the primordial wisdom only nature can gift us,
in the tiniest acts of charity and kindness,
in the unfurling of a new leaf and unfolding of new love,
in knowing the Universe has our back.

Serenity, in fact, is everywhere we turn, just like its prayer.
It is simply up to each of us to summon it forth every day
to keep the broken world from breaking us.

Maybe old Frank was on to something. Serenity now!

Nine-One-One

***

The wooden beams crisscrossing the ceiling come to life, moaning and cracking, softly at first and then louder and louder until *boom!* one of them explodes, sending fire balls and splinters raining down. *Incoming* I think as I dodge the hailstorm and sprint to the opposite corner of the room and slide down the wall to regroup. I had fled the blaze as it spread through the building, literally running for my life with the flames in—yes!—hot pursuit and finally taking refuge in this room, the only one not burning. But now the fire is coming through three walls and the ceiling and my escape is cut off. Panic savagely grips my chest and throat. Firefighters in the building are calling *Is anyone here? Is anyone here?* but cannot hear my screams for help over the blare of the fire alarm and sirens outside. The heat is scorching and I sink lower and lower seeking respite but none is to be had. The smoke entwines me, I can't breathe, I begin to choke . . .

***

. . . and I'm still choking as my eyes fly open in the early dawn light. I bolt out of bed to survey the scene in my bedroom. No smoke or fire, just my dog softly snoring at the foot of the bed and a spring breeze ruffling the curtains on an open window. Sanity begins to return. *That dream again,* I mumble to myself. Lately, as the state of the world has turned so black, my recurring dream of being trapped in a burning building has been visiting more often. *No wonder*, I think as I settle back in bed. The perennial angst of human existence has gone on steroids. Atrocity, hatred, treachery, deceit, war, suffering, destruction everywhere you look. No one is immune to it, and at times it truly feels like we're all trapped in a doomed world. I often think of that song Billy Joel wrote—*we didn't start the fire, it was always burning since the world's been turning . . .* Part of me wants to believe that we can still turn this thing around, that we just need to learn to be more humane, more caring, more enlightened, more aligned with God, more something in how we live. An uphill climb, but every spiritual and religious path says it can be done. *I have faith,* I say to myself, almost as a mantra. *I believe we can put out the fire.*

***

But as I get up to make my coffee, I can feel the heat rising.

Bombus

she grants life
a tiny goddess
flitting here there
and back again
buzzing and flying
erratically

bumbling about
and hence her name
the bumble bee
of genus bombus
which does her
little justice
given her mission
to seed creation
and enrich the world

which she attends to
with full force
since her lifespan
of a mere month or so
gives her little time
to bestow her gifts
and leaves her
wings ragged
at her final landing

she is admired
for her industry
and harmony
with her peers
something we could
learn so much from
if only we listened
but we don't
because arrogance
closes our ears

always ready to
impart her magic
she bumbles on
blissfully unaware
she is one of a
dying breed
who cannot
save us from

ourselves

War of the Worlds

tears
    sting my face
    jaggedly roll down
    pause on the arc of my jaw
    then reach for my flannel shirt
    to leave dark ugly stains

grief
    holds me hostage
    as I am forced to watch
    the subjugation of all my relations
    to the apathy avarice and amorality
    of the grim human race

guilt
    blazes in me
    for the role I inescapably play
    in the shameful ravaging
    of a miraculous verdant orb
    that stands apart in its cosmic grace

fear
    clutches my throat
    as the ecosystem teeters
    and species struggle

to avoid going dark
in the fossil record of our memories

rage
darkens my heart
as we fiddle while the planet burns
and fritter away our innate brilliance
on amassing billions of bitcoins
and preening on the red carpet

peace
dawns over me
with the certainty that Terra will prevail
that she will shake us off like fleas
and abide in renewed glory
even if we most deservedly do not

And One More

Poetry is when an emotion has found its thought and the thought has found words.

— Robert Frost

Poems

A haiku tribute to poetry

poems write themselves
let the humble poet know
when the time has come

poems and poets
then entwine and dance the words
onto the blank slate

each needs the other
for the poem to be birthed
from its mystic womb

the newborn poem
steps forth with its own heartbeat
what a miracle

its words pirouette
in the depths of the reader
spark new ways to be

truth leaps from the page
for those who want to see it
stills the inner lies

more meaning unveiled
each time the poem is read
a gift from above

poems go unread
by so many so often
such a tragedy

www.ingramcontent.com/pod-product-compliance
Lightning Source LLC
LaVergne TN
LVHW051014080826
845145LV00009B/2616